SONGWRITING SHORTCUTS

FOR THE

NATIVE AMERICAN FLUTE

JONNY LIPFORD
AWARD-WINNING RECORDING ARTIST AND EDUCATOR

jonnylipfordmusic.com

Published by Jonny Lipford
PO Box 981, Marion, Iowa 52302
www.jonnylipfordmusic.com

For information contact: info@JonnyLipfordMusic.com
Cover by Jonny Lipford
ISBN: 978-1-71661-595-5
Imprint: Lulu.com

PRAISE

Absolutely incredible at teaching and guiding people through skills and techniques around the Native American Flute. Expert at what he does. Very grateful to have found Jonny!

-Travin N.

Jonny Lipford's "Getting Unstuck" class was packed full of tips and tricks for moving forward when learning the Native American flute. He included an impressive 16 page illustrated workbook and followed up with additional resources. Jonny didn't miss a step and his middle name is "generous"! I highly recommend him as a master teacher and musician.

-Linda J.

Clear, supportive, encouraging teacher. Very generous with sharing his knowledge and passion for the Native American flute. Totally recommend for all things NAF!

-Amber F.

JL is the best teacher I have found, his classes/workshops are well planned, clear, and always interesting and informative. I have learned a lot from Jonny and plan to keep on with it. He really addresses not only the technical side of playing, but the cognitive and emotive sides as well and how to successfully mix them all together.

-Judith K.

DEDICATION

This book is dedicated to each and every one of my flute students.

Thank you for trusting me with your flute journey.

You have taught me so much and inspired me to capture my songwriting process so that it may be shared with those seeking to write their own songs with the Native American flute.

If you're reading this...
know that you are capable of amazing things!

You got this!

Music gives a soul to the universe, wings to the mind, flight to the imagination and life to everything.

PLATO

CONTENTS

DIGITAL RESOURCES

As you go through this book, you will find hyperlinks and exercises that may be challenging to access. I've built a secret page on my website where you can access these materials all in one place.

YouTube videos have been embedded directly into the page and there are several PDFs that you can download and print off as many copies as you need.

Get full access by visiting me at:

http://bit.ly/jl-SSR

WHY I WROTE THIS BOOK

When I began my flute journey in 2002, there were very few resources available for the Native American flute. In fact, social media and YouTube didn't exist, there were no classes, workshops or flute circles near me, and no books to read or videos on flute playing. I was discouraged, but determined. The one thing I did have access to was recordings. I listened to so much flute music and took a spin at trying to mimic the various embellishments I heard. While I was learning more about my flute and how to get some cool sounds out of it, I was still feeling unfulfilled. I was eager to learn more, but had nowhere to turn. My two biggest hang ups were how to play vibrato and how to write a song with the Native American flute.

Fast forward many years and I have written and published more than 200 songs spanning across 16 award-winning titles and now work with flute players all over the world to help them achieve their goals in flute playing. In working with hundreds of students, I've come to realize that, while each person has a very unique path with the flute, there are many common areas in which they get stuck. The same was true for me. That's why I put together this e-book. I wanted to broaden my reach and help as many flute players as possible turn on the music inside them so they can share it with the masses. One of the hardest areas in this process is capturing it. I hear time and time again, while playing improv or just noodling around on the flute, you came up with a cool melody or motif and you have no idea how to replicate it.

Photo of Jonny Lipford playing at sunset in Arizona

WHO DID I WRITE THIS BOOK FOR?

YOU

The everyday flute player looking to get more out of their Native American flute.

There's a high percentage of folks playing the Native American flute who don't read music or know anything about music theory. **And that's okay; you don't necessarily need to.** In this book, I'm going to give you some ideas around how you can capture those little melodies, archive them and then provide some framework so you can arrange a complete 3-4 minute song of your own.

I'm excited for you to begin, or perhaps continue, this part of your journey with the Native American flute.

You. *Can.* Make. Music.

Let's get started!

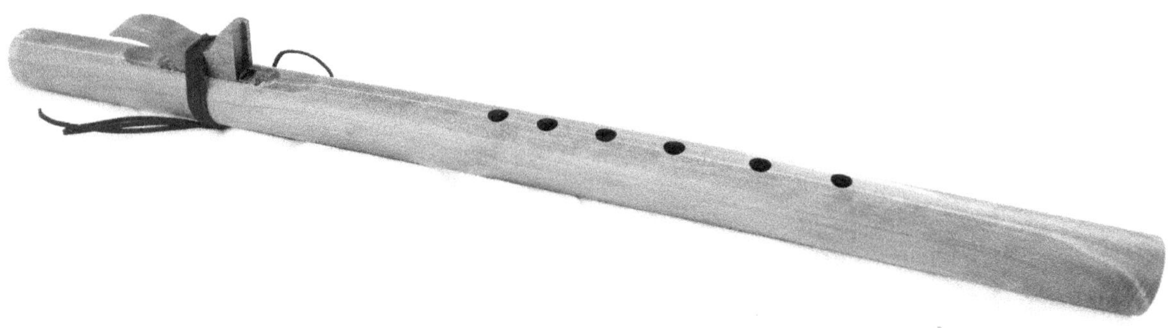

Flute shown is an E4 flute made by Butch Hall • Find Your Next Flute at bit.ly/jl-nafs

ELEMENTS OF MUSIC

Before we dive into templates for writing songs with your Native American flute, let's first go over some common vocabulary that we see when referring to music and how it's used in your song, specifically, songs written on and for the Native American flute.

NOTES

Notes are more than symbols denoting musical sound; they are the building blocks of written music which represent the pitch and duration of that sound.

TEMPO

Tempo is the speed or pace given for a piece of music.

Did you know?

BPM stands for **Beats Per Minute**. This is typically what tempo is written in. If you see 60 BPM, it means 60 beats per minute.

RHYTHM

Rhythm, in music, is the placement of sounds in time. In its most general sense, rhythm is an ordered alternation of contrasting elements. The notion of rhythm also occurs in other arts (i.e., poetry, painting, sculpture, and architecture) as well as in nature (i.e., biological rhythms).

PITCH

Pitch is the quality of a sound governed by the rate of vibrations producing it, the degree of highness or lowness of a tone.

MELODY

Melodies often consist of one or more musical phrases or motifs and are usually repeated throughout a composition in various forms.

MOTIF

A motif is a short melodic or rhythmic idea that is usually manipulated and repeated throughout a piece of music.

ELEMENTS OF MUSIC

cont'd...

PHRASE

A phrase refers to the notes contained in one breath.

EMBELLISHMENT

Embellishments add spice to your playing. You may also know them as flourishes or ornamentations. These directly impact the notion of "how" you play a song, rather than "what" the song consists of.

ARRANGEMENT

This refers to the formula or overall layout of your song.

SPACE

Space is one of the most under-used elements of a song, namely in solo Native American flute playing. Far too often, I hear flute players rush through a song without giving the listener a break. Space provides an opportunity for the listener to truly absorb the music and for you to regain your breath.

ENERGY

Energy refers to the mood or emotion of the piece that you're playing/writing.

DYNAMICS

Dynamics refer to the application of said energy in your song. Usually we think of dynamics as playing more loudly or more softly. Working with volume and vibrato is a great way to show an increase or decrease in emotion or energy. You should be writing and playing music in a way that creates *hills and valleys*, making it more interesting for the listener.

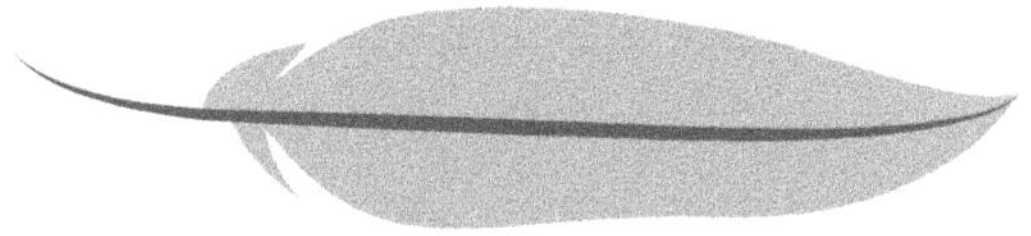

PARTS OF A SONG

Most of these definitions are used to explain more lyrical music; however, we can appreciate these meanings and with a little tweaking, realize them as part of an instrumental song.

INTRO

The intro of your song is much like the first handshake or hug you exchange when meeting someone. You're establishing the demeanor and feeling of your song. *Is it familiar and calm? Warm and inviting? Perhaps bold and expressive?*

Many key elements of your song become established in the intro including the key, tempo, energy and rhythmic feel. Your intro can include hints of your main parts in the song: for example, starting with a motif or short melody later heard in your song. You could also create an intro that has no material later found in your song.

It sounds backwards, but you won't often begin with an intro in songwriting!

Did you know?

In most lyrical music, the intro is usually instrumental, containing a motif or melody that is later found in the song.

VERSE

The verse is where we find out more information about the song and your verse should be made up of several phrases. These phrases are like lines in a poem, and the verses are like stanzas in a poem. The verses may be different than the chorus and often have less energy or complexity.

There are generally multiple verses in a lyrical song and each verse typically has different lyrics while the melody will likely be the same. We get more information about the story with each additional verse.

With instrumental music, we can't necessarily play the same exact melody over and over, as that would become incredibly boring for the listener. However, we should focus on **how** we deliver the second verse and **how** it contrasts from the one we just played. A common way to do this is by leveraging your selection of embellishments and modulating your volume and vibrato.

PARTS OF A SONG

cont'd...

PRE-CHORUS

The pre-chorus usually lives between the verse and the chorus and its main job is to set up the chorus to be something memorable. You can use this area to build up a little tension and let the chorus resolve it for maximum effect. The length of a pre-chorus is for you to determine as there is no correct length.

Did you know?

It's best to use a pre-chorus in solo flute playing if your verse and chorus are quite different and you feel that jumping from one to the other is too much contrast. The pre-chorus can then act as a **connector** from your verse to your chorus.

CHORUS

This is where your main melody should live. Often referred to as a "hook," the chorus is considered to be the most important part of your song. This is the earworm, the part of a song that you just can't get out of your head.

BRIDGE

The majority of songs contain some combination of a verse, chorus, and a bridge developed into an overall song structure. Songwriters often place their catchiest musical ideas in the chorus and their most evocative lyrical ideas in the verses. However, the bridge provides songwriters with the opportunity to insert a musical change of pace into a song. This is a great opportunity to increase or decrease the "energy" in your song.

OUTRO

This is the conclusion of the story you've been telling with your song. In many cases, you can simply rehash your intro, or perhaps you want to repeat the "hook" of your song but with less energy. You could also end with fading out this part or by using more energy and closing with a Yip or Bark. Try not to linger on the outro too long. Keep this part succinct.

LET'S TALK ABOUT

FORMULAS

From here, we will give each part of a song a **"label"** so that we can easily write them down without having to use the whole word. This is very common for musicians when they are speaking about the "form" of any given song.

VERSE = A
PRE-CHORUS = PRE
CHORUS = B
BRIDGE = C
INTRO = i
OUTRO = o

On the next page, I'll share one of the most common formulas used in pop, rock and country music, as well as the 8 songwriting formulas that you can employ in your flute playing. From there, we will look at strategies on how you can transform your short melodies into something longer like a 3-4 minute song!

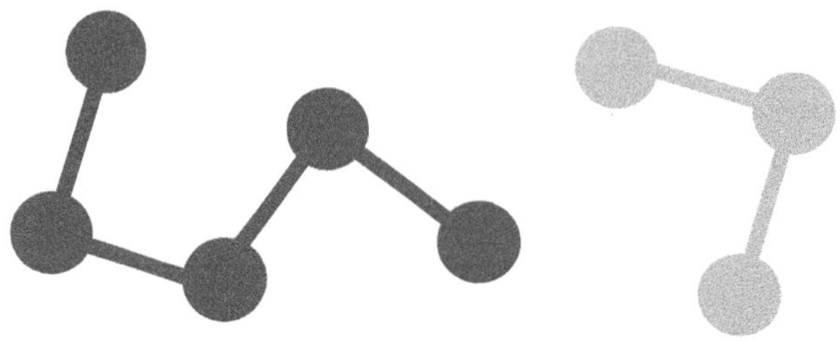

THE BEST FORMULA?

Friedemann Findeisen, author of ***The Addiction Formula***, talks about this one specific formula behind the majority of the Top 40 songs playing on pop, rock and country radio stations. Here's the formula:

Intro, Verse, Verse cont'd, Pre-Chorus, Chorus, Verse, Pre-Chorus, Chorus, Bridge, Bridge cont'd, Chorus, Chorus, Outro

This looks complicated. Let's use labels to see the form more clearly.

i - A1 - A2 - PRE - B1 - A1 - PRE - B1 - C1 - C2 - B1 - B2 - o

i	A1	A2	PRE	B1	A1	PRE	B1	C1	C2	B1	B2	o
Intro	*Verse*	*Verse cont'd*	*Pre-Chorus*	*Chorus*	*Verse*	*Pre-Chorus*	*Chorus*	*Bridge*	*Bridge cont'd*	*Chorus*	*Chorus cont'd*	*Outro*

THE NUMBERS?

When you see the number "1" or "2" behind one of the letters representing a part of the song, it means that it repeats. Don't forget about working with energy and dynamics! Perhaps the first time through it is more simple with fewer embellishments and the second time through might have more volume, heavier vibrato and/or more exaggerated embellishments.

Did you know?

As you look at the various formulas laid out on the next page, you'll notice that there are repeating parts (labels) in every song. This means that you really only have to aim to write about 1-2 minutes of music for a 3-4 minute song!

The formula above may not work that well with solo Native American flute music, but I bet it would work if we were to have more instruments playing with us. This would allow more opportunity for dynamics, harmony, energy, tension and resolve. Unfortunately, there isn't ONE magical formula that is king when it comes to our genre of music, but let's take a look at some that would work!

FLUTE SONG FORMULAS

For the sake of simplifying this process, I'm not including any Pre-Choruses (pre's), Intros (i's) or Outros (o's) in the following formulas. Feel free to add these to your song as you see fit. When writing a song, we don't typically start with the intro, even though it's the first part played in a song!

SIMPLE FORMULAS	COMPLEX FORMULAS
A - A - A	A - B - C - B - A
A - B - A	A - B - A - C - B
A - B - A - B	A - B - A - C - B - A
A - A - B - A*	A - B - A - B - C - B

**Denotes one of the most popular song formulas. We'll work with this formula later in the book!*

SIMPLE FORMULA EXAMPLES

Let's see how these formulas sound in a song. Just like our flutes, please know that each song has its own personality. These are simply listed as an example.

A - A - A ***Amazing Grace | Jonny Lipford***

All of these sections are the same. We'll talk more about this particular song a bit later when discussing energy and dynamics.
Listen here: https://youtu.be/sK0ARfRA6sI

A - B - A ***Twinkle Twinkle Little Star | Jewel***

A section starts at **0:04** with: "*Twinkle twinkle little star*"
B section starts at **1:17** with: "*In the dark blue sky you keep*"
A section starts at **1:42** with: "*As your bright and tiny spark*"

In this version, Jewel finishes off the song by resolving with a part of A and creating a spaced out outro. Listen here: https://youtu.be/J-YbqUYdgrs

A - B - A - B ***Fly Me to the Moon | Frank Sinatra***

A section starts at **0:07** with: "*Fly me to the moon*"
B section starts at **0:25** with: "*In other words, hold my hand*"
A section starts at **0:39** with: "*Fill my heart with song*"
B section starts at **0:55** with: "*In other words, please be true*"

This form happens rather quickly. After these sections, the song wraps up with a repeated B section and outro: https://youtu.be/ZEcqHA7dbwM

A - A - B - A ***Somewhere Over the Rainbow | Judy Garland***

A section starts at **0:01** with: "*Somewhere over the rainbow*"
A section starts at **0:22** with: "*Somewhere over the rainbow*"
B section starts at **0:44** with: "*Some day I'll wish upon a star*"
A section starts at **1:12** with: "*Somewhere over the rainbow*"

Much like Fly Me To The Moon, after these sections, the song wraps up with a repeated B section: https://youtu.be/PSZxmZmBfnU

COMPLEX FORMULA EXAMPLES

These next two song formulas are quite complicated. They may or may not work with your solo flute pieces. Both songs feature instrumental parts, which give a break from the vocal. When looking at any one of these songs, imagine that your flute is the vocal part. What fills the instrumental parts then?

A - B - A - C - B - A ***Every Breath You Take | The Police***

A section starts at **0:16** with: "*Every breath you take*"
B section starts at **0:48** with: "*Oh can't you see*"
A section starts at **1:05** with: "*Every move you make*"
C section starts at **1:23** with: "Since you've gone"
B section starts at **2:15** with: "*Oh can't you see*"
A section starts at **2:35** with: "*Every move you make*"

The song demonstrates a rather long and interesting outro:
https://youtu.be/OMOGaugKpzs

A - B - A - B - C - B ***What's Love Got To Do With It | Tina Turner***

A section starts at **0:20** with: "*You must understand*"
B section starts at **0:53** with: "*What's love got to do with it*"
A section starts at **1:12** with: "*It may seem to you*"
B section starts at **1:44** with: "*What's love got to do with it*"
C section starts at **2:04** with an instrumental, lyrics come in at **2:23**
B section starts at **2:40** with: "*What's love got to do with it*"

For the outro on this song, the B section is repeated and faded: https://youtu.be/oGpFcHTxjZs

THE THREE-STEP PROCESS

When students are learning a new song or writing a song for the first time, I typically break it down into three parts.

THE WHAT

Start with **the notes only**. If there's a part of the song that creates a hang-up, typically due to an awkward fingering combination, slow down and take your time. Name your problem areas and keep working through them. Don't worry about anything else during this time.

1

THE TRANSITION

Once you have a good grip on the notes and have developed some muscle memory around what notes come next, turn your focus to the **timing and rhythm** of the song. Those same problem areas might show up again here, but keep working through the sticky parts.

2

THE HOW

I see many flute players starting here before they're ready. **Embellishments** should be the last area you focus on. I'll go one step further and add **volume, vibrato and space** to this list, as well.

These are the elements that will take your song to the next level!

3

On the next page, I'm going to share with you how shifting your intent to "how" you play a song makes an incredible impact on a listener.

SHIFTING GEARS TO THE HOW

Why is it that sometimes when we hear songs like the national anthem or Amazing Grace, we become overwhelmed by emotion? Other times, we feel nothing at all.

It's all in **how** the musician delivered the song to us.

Amazing Grace is a very common song played on the Native flute. This song uses the "A-A-A" formula, which, in turn, leaves it feeling quite repetitive. Any time I perform this song as a solo Native American flute song, I try to add interest for the listener by playing it the following way:

A1 Slow, simple and clean, lacking a lot of embellishments. I pretend this is my intro.

A2 Because the listener has already heard the melody, I need to spruce it up a bit. I'll add some embellishments (pop, bending, tonguing, etc.) and I won't sustain notes for as long.

A3 This is the last time through the form, I'm going to vary my rate of vibrato and volume, in addition to adding embellishments. I may hold notes at the end of phrases a little longer. I'll really slow down for the last phrase. This helps the listener know that the end of the song is near.

ENERGY & DYNAMICS

A1 A2 A3

This is where I started to slow down, holding notes longer during the last phrases, hinting at the end.

Listen! Hear me play Amazing Grace exactly this way: https://youtu.be/sK0ARfRA6sI

USING ENERGY AND DYNAMICS

with your solo Native American flute songs

No matter where you are in your flute journey, it's important to work with breath control. This is some of the most crucial work we can do with our woodwind instruments. When I work with flute players for the first time, I often give them an exercise called "**Earth to Sky.**" In this exercise they will play each note of the basic scale as softly as possible and gradually increase their volume on that note until it's as loud as they can play it.

Why soft then loud?

It's natural to start out loud and fade as we run out of breath, but that fade isn't necessarily intentional. It's a result of running out of breath. When you do it the opposite way, you're really training your muscles and body to control your breath and the volume going into your flute.

The reason I promote this rather simple exercise is because it's a great practice warm up. Think of it as stretching before running. This one simple exercise also shows you how much volume you have to play with and that your song or playing doesn't have to have the same volume level throughout.

When you do increase or decrease volume, you also sharpen or flatten the pitch of the note respectively, however, I'm not too worried about this right now. The most important thing is that you're starting to play with breath control and manipulating the volume of your flute.

Please note, every flute is different and you will most likely experience a great deal of difference in back pressure amongst your flutes.

Take action!

Try the Earth to Sky exercise on your flute. It's a good idea to do this at the beginning of your practice time to warm up!

PHRASING

A simple way to define phrasing is that it refers to the notes that are contained in one breath. Phrasing goes beyond just playing the notes and for the sake of this exercise, we're going to examine written language. For example, you wouldn't read each word as its own unit, rather you would group the words to form an idea of inflection and tone.

If I were to recite this poem and speak each word as its unit, it would come out choppy like this:

Roses | are | red - Violets | are | blue
I | play | the | flute - and | so | do | you

That sounds robotic, boring and flat. How would you naturally say it?

Roses are red, Violets are blue
I play the flute, and so do you

Take a look at where the comma is. This is a really good indicator of where a breath might be. Let's dissect one more time, this time using **phrasing marks** above each phrase to give you a better understanding of what we're after here:

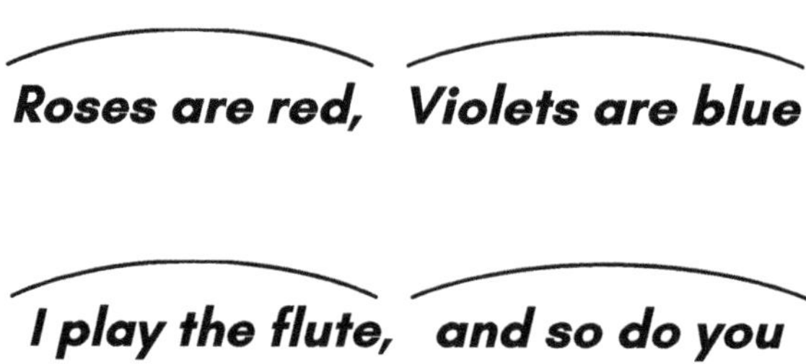

POETIC PLAYING

Poetic playing is an intentional measure that you can use in your songwriting and improv sessions to dramatically improve and balance your music. Often, when students are feeling stuck in their flute playing, I have them look at written language for inspiration. This can be in the form of poetry, lyrics, or devotions. When you find something that you resonate with, try to add music to it.

Treat each syllable of the words as a note and each natural breaking point as a breathing opportunity and/or a potential separation of phrases. Let's look at putting music to the poem we were working with earlier below.

PLAYING A SIMPLE POEM

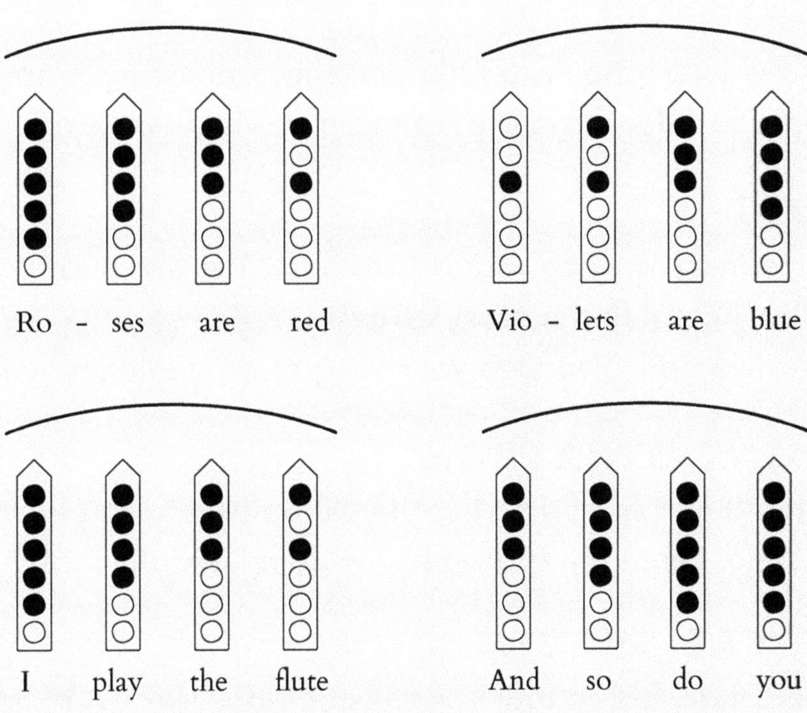

SONGWRITING TOOLKIT

This toolkit was designed for you to get the most out of your songwriting experience. While these applications and templates helped me early on in my songwriting efforts, they may not be the solution for you. I encourage you to take liberty and experiment with ways that work best for you!

Here's what you'll find in your toolkit:

CAPTURING TACTICS

Learn methods to capture your idea or melody before it even hits paper.

PHRASING PROMPTS

Sometimes our inspiration is a little dry. These phrasing prompts will give you a springboard for ideas and a parameter in which to work.

STORY SHEET

When you create a song on your Native flute, there's usually a reason...an intent...a story. You'll find a **story questionnaire** so you can work on fleshing out the narrative and introduce your song to an audience with confidence.

ARRANGEMENT STRATEGY

Transform those simple and short little melodies into something larger - a full-length song. Learn my strategies for doing exactly that!

BLANK NAF TAB SHEETS

You'll also have access to four varieties of Blank NAF TAB Sheets so you can physically write out your melody. You'll want to be sure to do this to get the most our of the arrangement strategy.

CAPTURING TACTICS

I hear it time and time again...

> "I just played something that I really liked, but I have no idea what I did so how can I do it again?"

To remedy this, I would suggest that you get in the habit of recording your practice and play sessions in some way. I know this may feel uncomfortable at first, but there's so much that you can capture in these moments.

RECORDING VS. FILMING

You can capture a fair bit of information by just recording yourself playing your flute, but it may not tell the whole picture. You can note what flute you're playing with, but as inspiration hits - and it will - you may not have a good enough trained ear to repeat what you've played without seeing where your fingers are on the flute. When you film yourself (in "selfie" mode), you can see where your hands are on the flute and capture the melody you're working with.

What if you don't like something about this session?

Delete it.

But! If there's some nugget of goodness, play it back and try to replicate it as many times as you can, even if it's a 10-20 second melody. Try to set yourself up to record only that part and save it in a folder on your computer or in your phone. Cloud storage is preferred so you will have access to it no matter what happens to your phone or computer. You're on your way to transforming that 10-20 second idea into a full-length song!

PHRASING PROMPTS

Let's expand on the idea of playing "poetically" with your flute. In the following exercises, I have provided a note for you to start and end each phrase with. You can play ***as few as two or as many as eight notes*** between the starting and ending notes. Just keep in mind that each line is a phrase, which translates into one connected breath. Focus on playing in a way that you only have to take a breath between phrases. You don't need to use ALL the breath from your initial inhale. In fact, you may need to exhale before inhaling again for the next phrase. ***For the sake of this exercise***, imagine that these phrases belong in groups of four, shown with brackets to contain them.

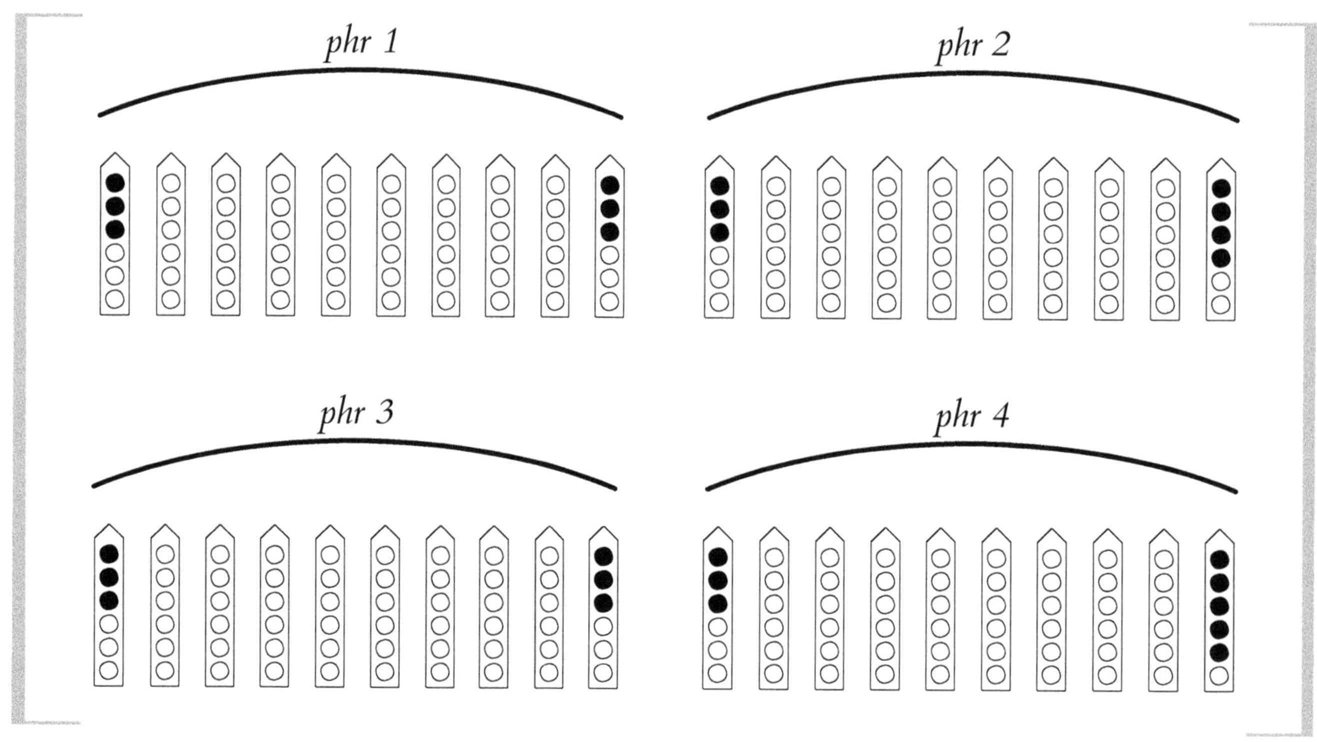

Helpful tip!

The last note in each phrase is arguably the most important note for this exercise. Make sure that you have enough breath to play that note fully by the time you get there, so your phrase doesn't end sounding weak or frail. Remember, you don't have to use all eight blank diagrams between, but they are there for you if you need them.

PHRASING PROMPTS

cont'd...

Let's continue our work with the next series of phrasing prompts by playing improv between the starting and ending notes. Once you have something you really like, you can fill in the finger diagrams to solidify your melody or thought.

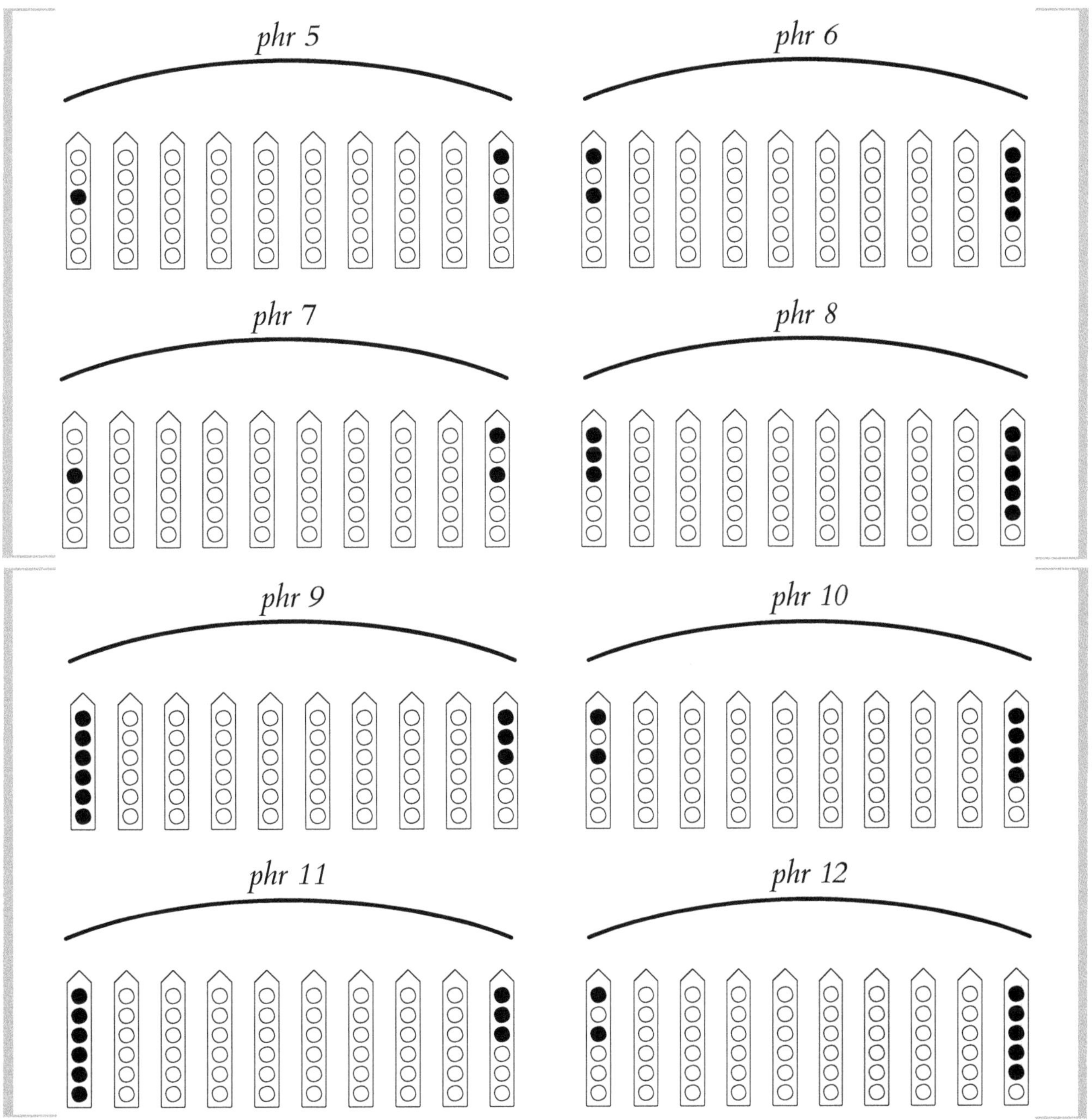

PUTTING IT TO PAPER

At the back of this book there are four Blank NAF TAB Sheets that you can print out and use when writing down your melody and arranging your song. You don't have to print all four, just choose one. Here are the varieties:

- Large: 4 rows with 16 notes *(larger diagrams)*
- Medium: 5 rows with 20 notes *(smaller diagrams)*
- Large Inverted: 4 rows with 16 notes *(larger diagrams, mouthpiece facing player)*
- Medium Inverted: 5 rows with 20 notes *(smaller diagrams, mouthpiece facing player)*

PENCIL IT IN

When you've decided on a Blank NAF TAB Sheet that you like and will do the job, print several copies to have on hand. From here we are going to take that little melody you came up with - no matter how short - and turn it into a physical copy.

Don't feel that you have to fill the whole page. The idea is to keep your sections to one page (or two if they are longer) so that you can lay them out and play through them. In the next step, we'll talk about how to arrange these little pieces into something larger. It's about to get a whole lot more fun!

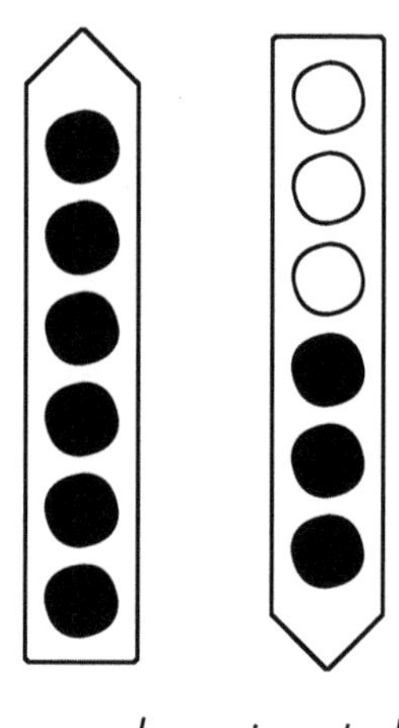

Circles that aren't filled are "open" holes while filled-in circles are "closed" holes.

Did you know?

When filling in the little circles of the finger diagrams, you can use a sharpie marker to dab the hole rather than an ink pen. It will save you time. This would be best for your final product. In the beginning start by using a pencil so that you can erase a mistake or modify your notes.

NOTE: Though the Blank NAF TAB Sheets show the staff, commonly seen in written music, I will not be addressing how to write the notes on that staff. Instead, we are focusing solely on finger diagrams for now. If you already read Nakai TAB you are welcome to use that feature. I will be creating a course for learning the Nakai TAB system in the future!

STORY QUESTIONNAIRE

Every song has a story. **What is yours?**

When I'm struggling to nail down a story about my song, I answer some basic questions like these:

What flute am I playing? ______________________________

Is there anything special about this flute? ______________________________

Is there a main theme or subject when I play this song? Y / N

If so, what? ______________________________

What is this subject doing? ______________________________

What is happening in the beginning? ______________________________

How does the subject feel? ______________________________

Think about what that emotion sounds like... what comes to mind? (i.e. slow, fast, playful, somber, etc...)

____

Is there a celebration, struggle or transformation happening? Y / N

If so, what? ______________________________

Is there some sort of conclusion for the subject? (e.g. reaching the end of the journey, being reunited, finding peace)

____

____

ARRANGEMENT STRATEGY

Early-on in my songwriting efforts, I developed this workflow to help me quickly and effectively arrange my pieces or melodies into a full song. You'll quickly see why I recommend keeping one section (i.e. "A" or "B") to its own piece of paper.

Once I've gone through the process of writing out my melodies on the Blank NAF TAB Sheets, I lay them out on the table and start to physically rearrange them.

Don't feel overwhelmed if you've come up with too many different ideas. Just try to group "like" ideas/sections together. These are ones that may be able to blend together. I have three different pieces below; **Bear Melody #1, Bear Melody #2** and **June 3rd Melody.**

These pieces of music are included later in the book. I've also added an unlisted video on YouTube where I am playing these sections so you can get an idea of how they sound. Here's a link: **https://youtu.be/pZnxIXJNEdM**

Let's see what we can do about bringing them together and making them into a complete song!

ARRANGEMENT STRATEGY
cont'd...

First, label these pieces as a section of our song. (e.g. A, B, C)

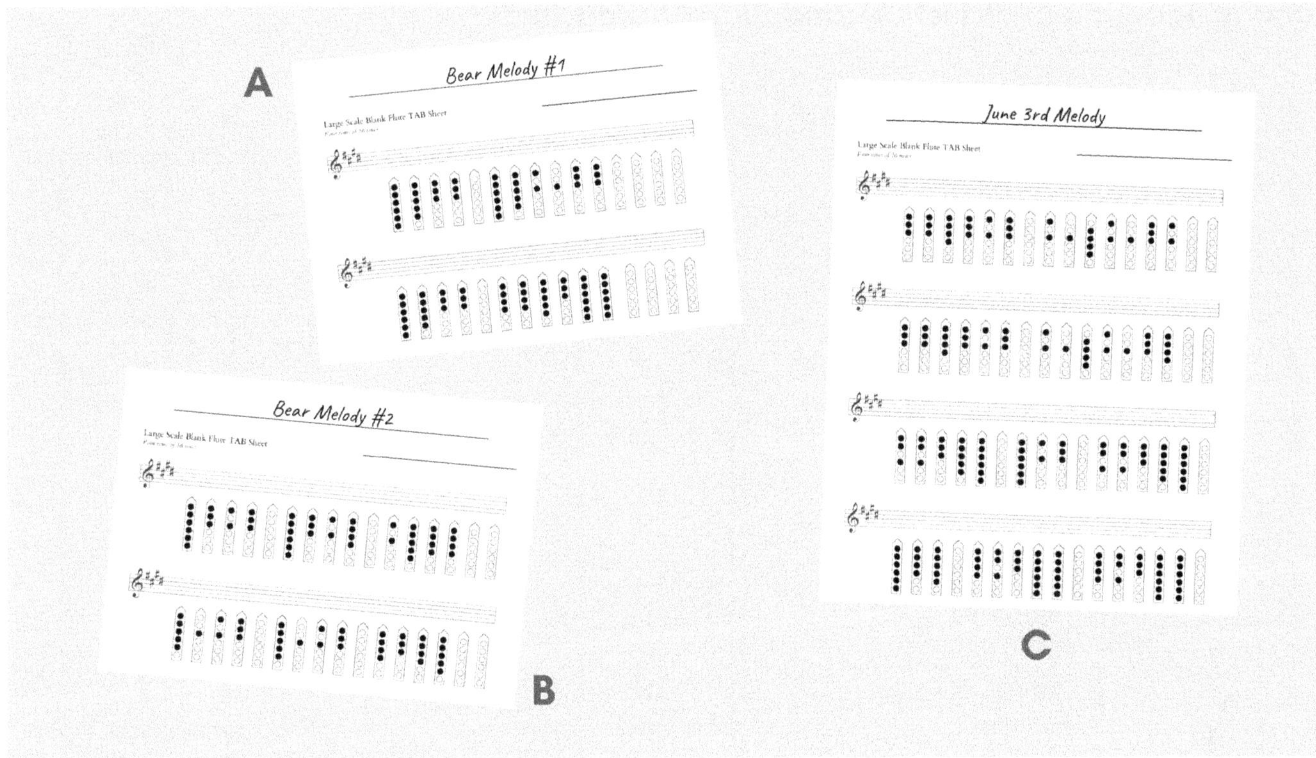

Now that we have labels for these pieces, let's pick a formula and try to play our song that way. Don't worry too much about the label you give each piece, the beauty of what you have created is that you can quickly rename and rearrange it into something different to try. Let's start with something simple. Let's try this one!

A - A - B - A

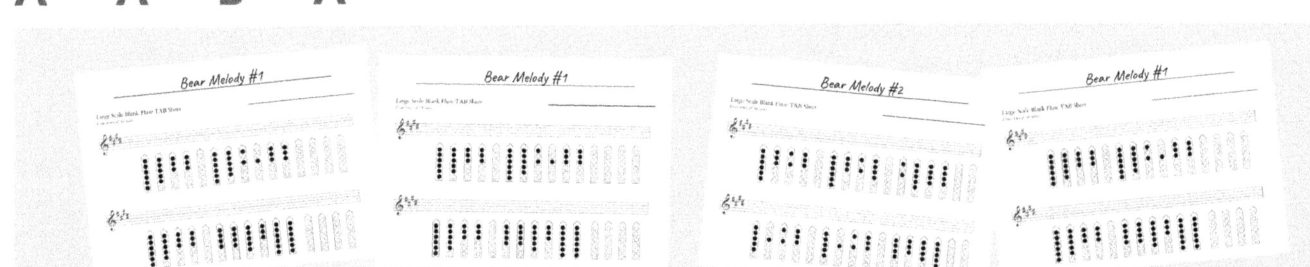

ARRANGEMENT STRATEGY

cont'd...

That arrangement put us under 2 minutes in total length. We still have a part that hasn't been used. Since "A" and "B" are similar, what if we were to combine them and re-label them as just "A" and turn "C" into "B"?

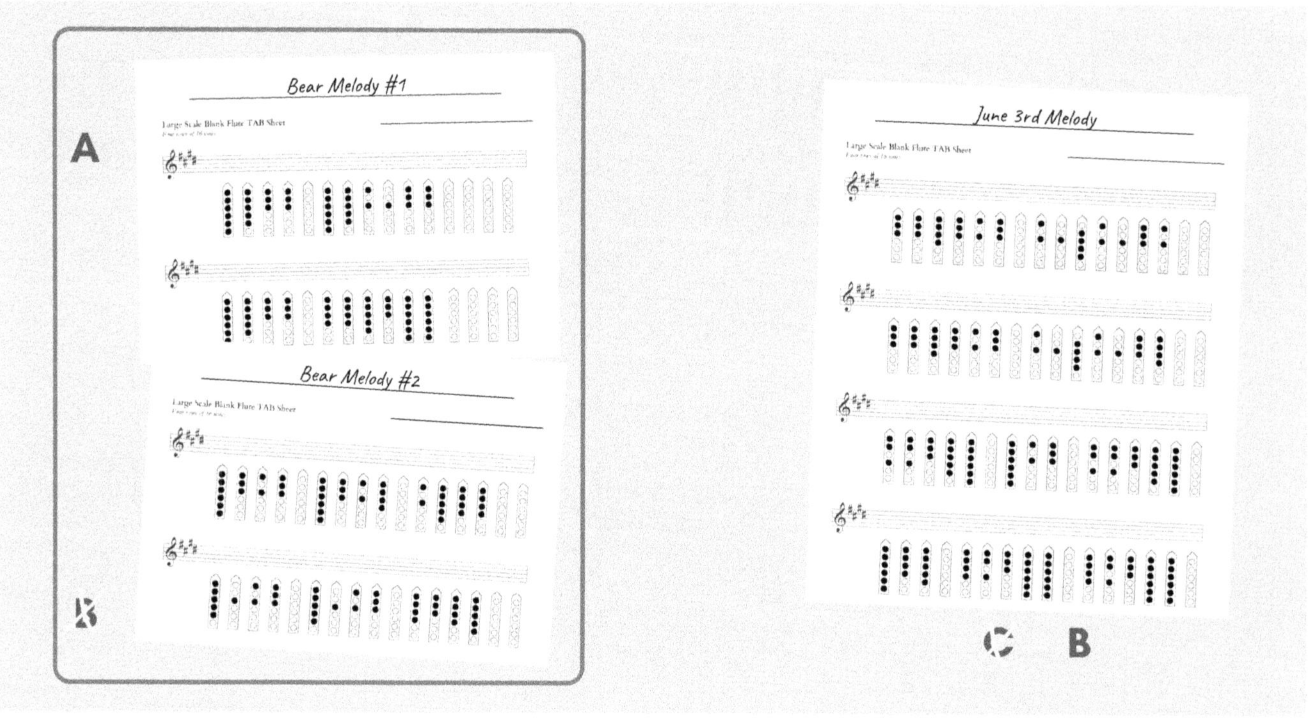

Since we re-labeled the pieces, let's try that same formula again!

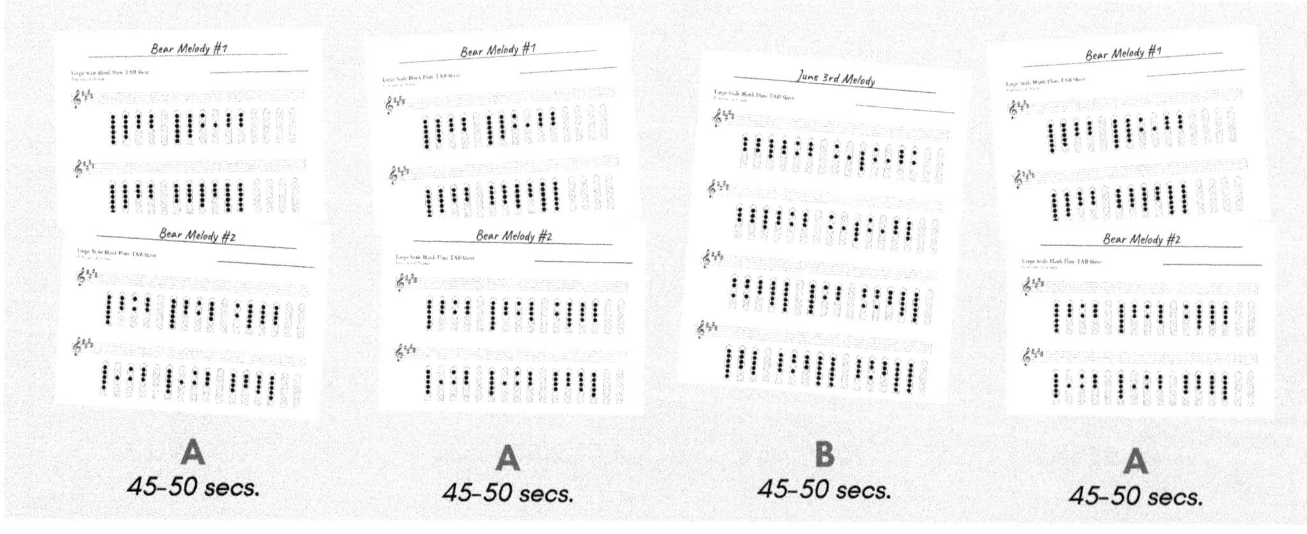

ARRANGEMENT STRATEGY

cont'd...

That arrangement not only sounds better and more interesting, it also puts the overall length of the song at around 3 minutes!

You can always try different formulas. There are several examples listed earlier in this book, but don't feel that you have to stick with one of these formulas. Music is expressive and personal and *your* music should reflect *you*.

The most important thing is that you're capturing and writing down your short melodies in order to do something greater with them.

Remember!

You don't have to write 4 minutes of music. Shoot for about 1-2 minutes of original ideas/music and know that sections in your arrangement will repeat.

SONGWRITING WORKFLOW

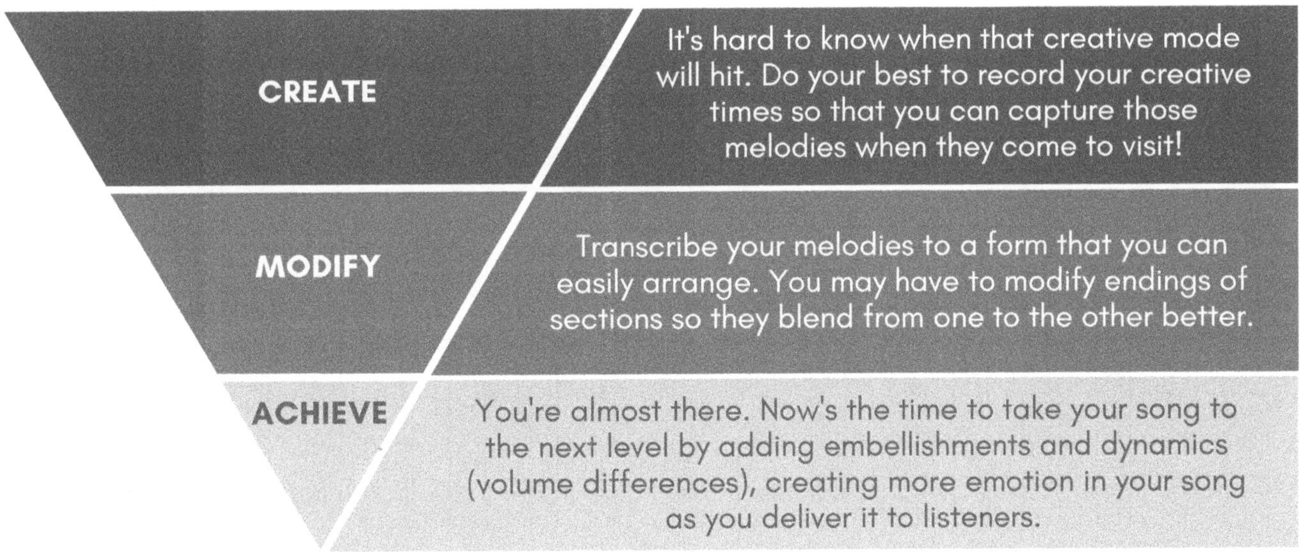

CREATE	It's hard to know when that creative mode will hit. Do your best to record your creative times so that you can capture those melodies when they come to visit!
MODIFY	Transcribe your melodies to a form that you can easily arrange. You may have to modify endings of sections so they blend from one to the other better.
ACHIEVE	You're almost there. Now's the time to take your song to the next level by adding embellishments and dynamics (volume differences), creating more emotion in your song as you deliver it to listeners.

Bear Melody #1

Large Scale Blank Flute TAB Sheet

Four rows of 16 notes

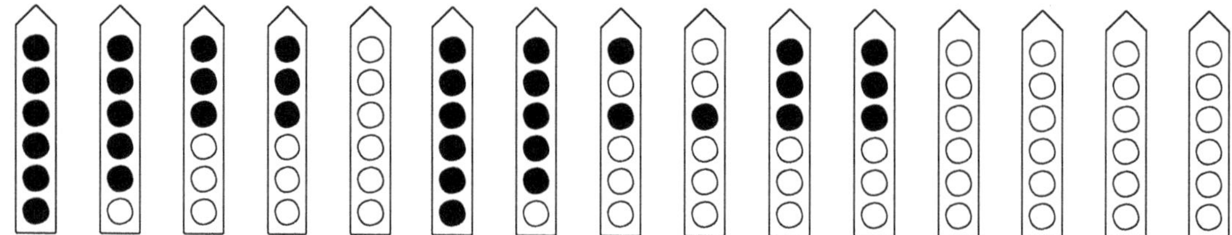

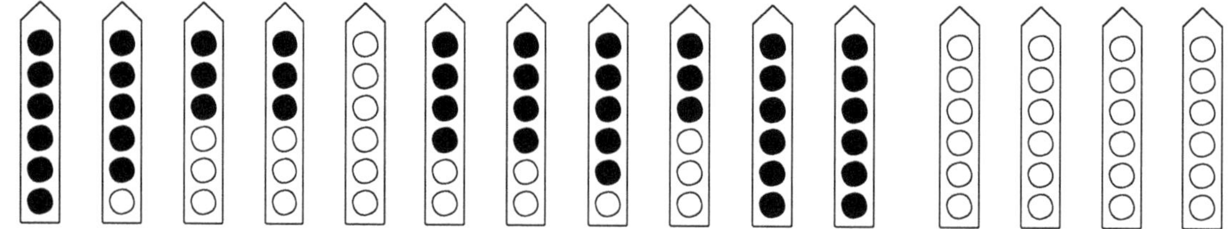

Helpful tip!

Skipping over one of the finger diagrams and leaving it blank between phrases (as shown above) helps me know when to breathe!

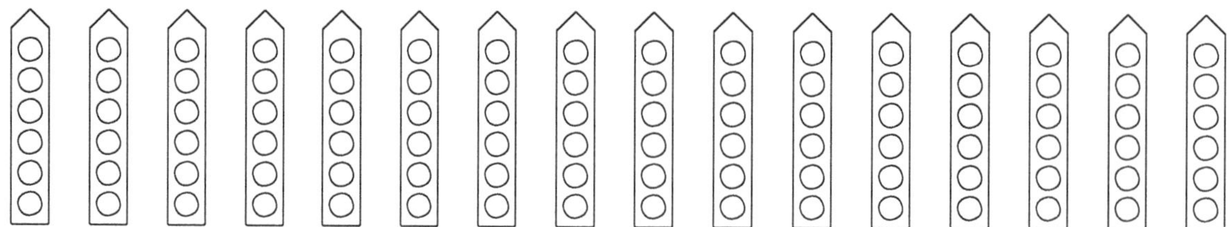

Blank staff template by Jonny Lipford • jonnylipfordmusic.com
Flute Font Diagrams courtesy of Robert Gatliff / Flute Tree Foundation • flutetree.org

Bear Melody #2

Large Scale Blank Flute TAB Sheet

Four rows of 16 notes

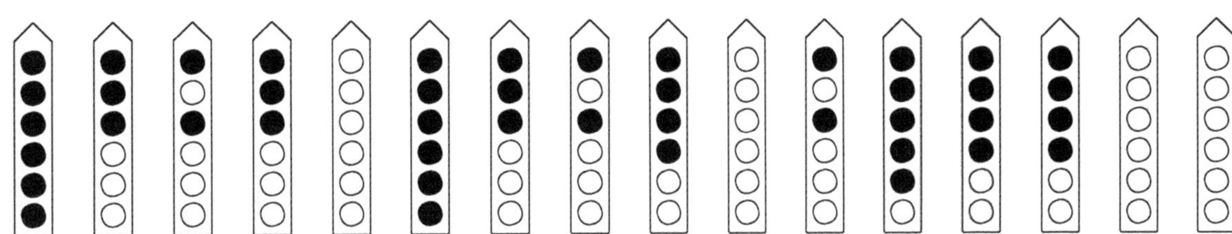

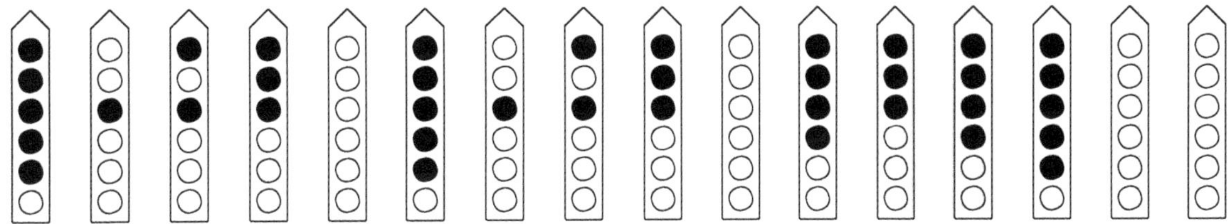

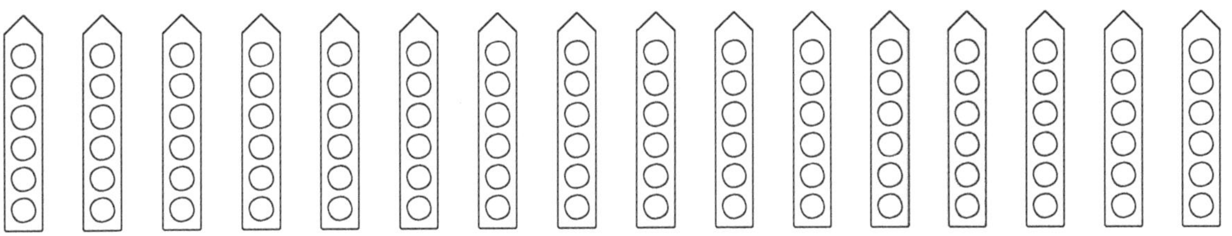

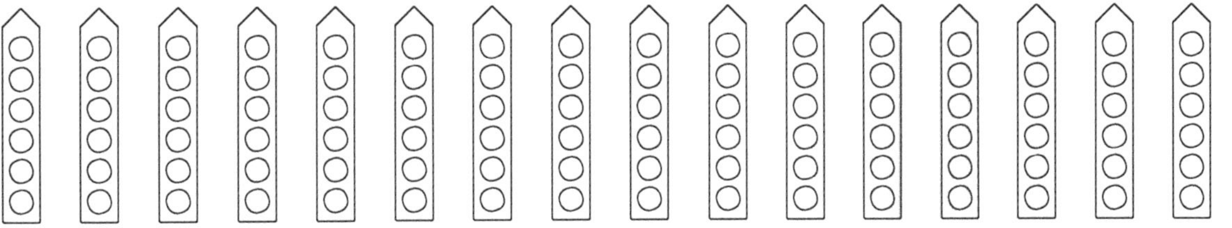

Blank staff template by Jonny Lipford • jonnylipfordmusic.com
Flute Font Diagrams courtesy of Robert Gatliff / Flute Tree Foundation • flutetree.org

June 3rd Melody

Large Scale Blank Flute TAB Sheet
Four rows of 16 notes

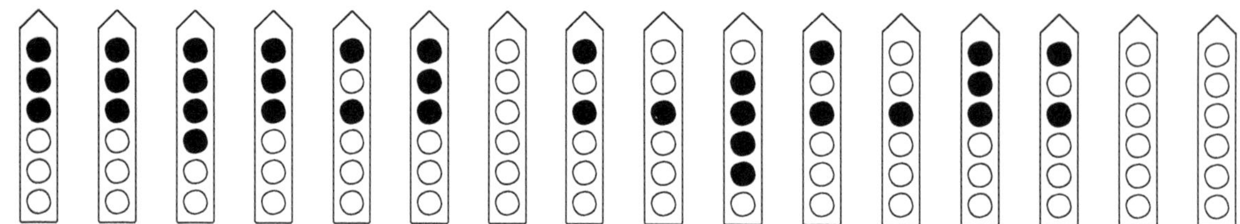

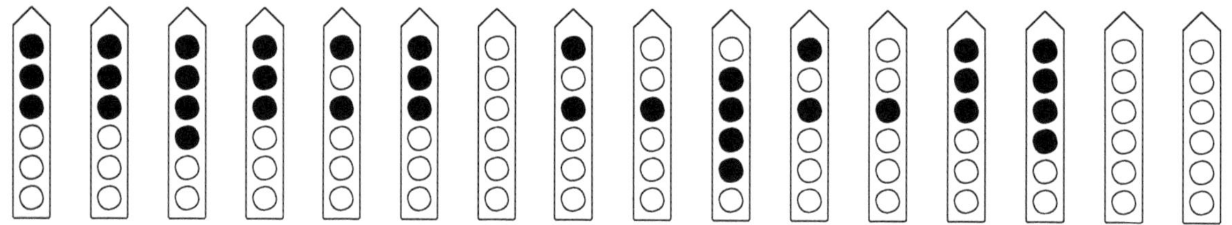

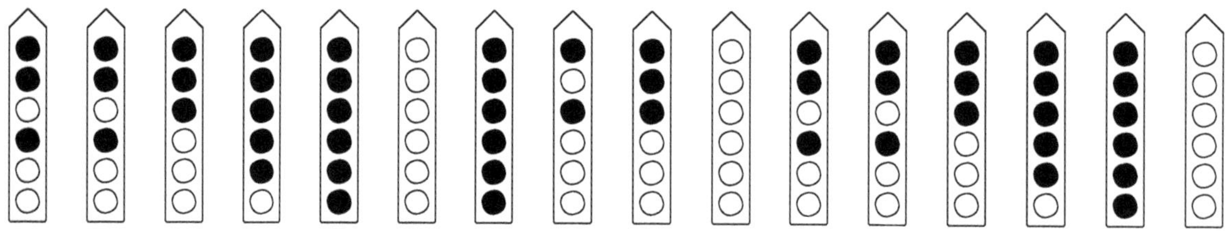

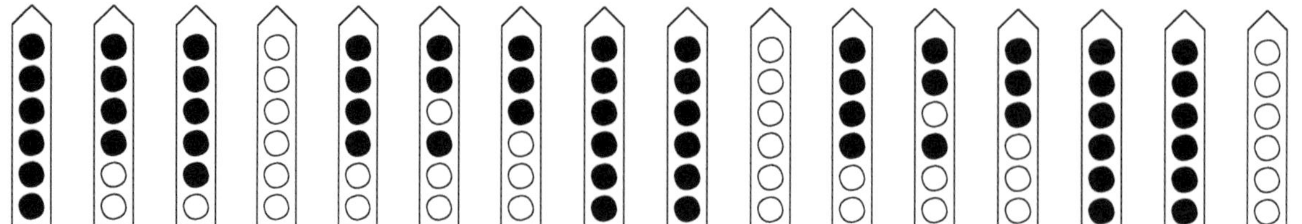

Blank staff template by Jonny Lipford • jonnylipfordmusic.com
Flute Font Diagrams courtesy of Robert Gatliff / Flute Tree Foundation • flutetree.org

Large Scale Blank Flute TAB Sheet

Four rows of 16 notes

Blank staff template by Jonny Lipford • jonnylipfordmusic.com
Flute Font Diagrams courtesy of Robert Gatliff / Flute Tree Foundation • flutetree.org

Medium Scale Blank Flute TAB Sheet

Five rows of 20 notes

Blank staff template by Jonny Lipford jonnylipfordmusic.com
Flute Font Diagrams courtesy of Robert Gatliff / Flute Tree Foundation flutetree.org

Large Scale Blank Flute TAB Sheet - Inverted Diagrams

Four rows of 16 notes

Blank staff template by Jonny Lipford • jonnylipfordmusic.com
Flute Font Diagrams courtesy of Robert Gatliff / Flute Tree Foundation • flutetree.org

Medium Scale Blank Flute TAB Sheet - Inverted Diagrams

Five rows of 20 notes

Blank staff template by Jonny Lipford jonnylipfordmusic.com
Flute Font Diagrams courtesy of Robert Gatliff / Flute Tree Foundation flutetree.org

CONCLUSION

I firmly believe that ***we all have music inside of us waiting to be unleashed***. This is why we sing, play, hum, whistle and tap our toes. However, if you aren't used to being expressive with music, you may need a little help learning how to get that music out.

My goal as an educator of Native American flutes is to help new and seasoned flute players find inspiration in their flute journey, so they feel motivated, creative and accomplished.

It's been a tremendous joy to work with so many flute players on tactics covered within this book. I hope that you feel inspired and ***start writing and sharing your own music with the Native American flute***.

I can't wait to hear what you come up with!

Peace,

ACKNOWLEDGMENTS

Writing a book is a lot of work and I see why it takes authors a long time to complete a project or to have the feeling of completion. There are so many ideas, discoveries, connections and, truly, distractions. This project is bigger than me. There are many people to thank but naming them all would take another book! With that said, there are a few key people who were directly involved in bringing this book to life...

I'm thankful for members of the **JL Tribe** who willingly show up to test new products, brainstorm ideas and proof read my caffeine-induced grammar mistakes. Thank you Sherry Bunch, Jill Geary, Stephen Padilla and Bill Schnippert for your dedication to this project!

I extend a harmonious hug to the many flute students that I've had the privilege to work with. Your curiousity and eagerness to advance your knowledge keeps me on my toes and pushes me to continue learning so I can be a stronger, more creative problem solver in the flute community.

A southern "howdy" to Julia & Robert Gatliff for their friendship and permission to use the flute diagrams in many projects. Check out their work at flutetree.org

To David Wood, who has been a sounding board, loyal friend and hard worker in producing sheet music. Your dedication to my vision has been unwavering and truly appreciated.

Last, but certainly not least, I am immensely grateful for my wife, Maria. I am in complete awe of the amount of faith you have in me. The world is a better place because you're in it, and my life is enriched because we're together. I love you!

ABOUT JONNY LIPFORD

Jonny Lipford is an award-winning musician of the modern Native American flute. With a mission of creating and composing music that pushes the boundaries of a once waning instrument, Jonny has awakened a new wave of flute players.

He received his first Native American flute in 2002 as a Christmas gift after hearing one in a cartoon at just 13 years of age. This instrument has provided a voice for Jonny and he has since made his mark in the industry as one of the most versatile and progressive musicians of the Native American flute.

His work as a recording artist includes more than 16 independent albums; many of which have received nominations and awards from prestigious music award organizations.

Not only is Jonny a well-decorated artist, he is also an award-winning instructor and has worked with hundreds of students to help them achieve their goals. His passion for connecting with and instructing students in a meaningful and charismatic way has led him to be one of the most sought-after instructors of the Native American flute.

Jonny is the co-founder and director of the Sweetgrass Flute & Nature Festival and Sweetgrass Flute School in Hiawatha, Iowa. He is based out of Cedar Rapids, Iowa, where he records and produces new music. His life-long goal continues to be writing and composing music that reaches new audiences and encourages inspiration within those who hear the voice of the flute.

OTHER RESOURCES

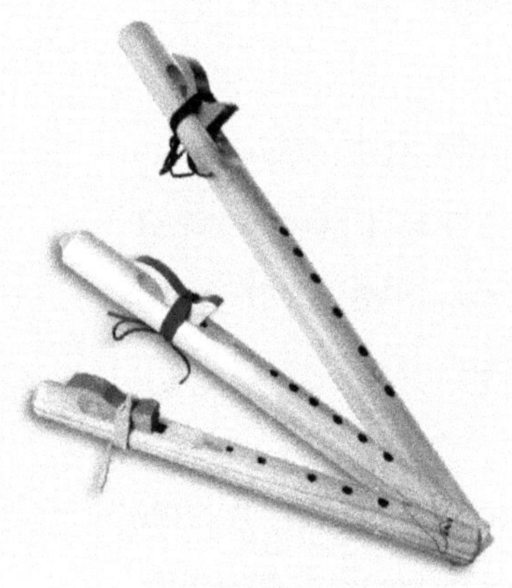

NATIVE AMERICAN-STYLE FLUTES

Having a well-tuned, responsive and reliable flute can make all the difference in the world when it comes to growing as a flute player. You'll find a curated selection of flutes on my website, along with sound samples and videos to help guide you.

Find a flute that's right for you at bit.ly/jl-nafs

ONLINE LEARNING RESOURCES

Whether you're just starting out on your journey with the Native American flute or you're a seasoned player, you'll find helpful resources on my website for perfecting your notes, getting out of a rut, learning new scales and more!

Strengthen your skills at bit.ly/jl-learn

SHEET MUSIC & BACKING TRACKS

Sheet music for popular, well-known songs and even JL originals is available for download. You'll also find a wide variety of backing tracks ranging from ambient to upbeat.

Learn a new song & get your groove on!

View sheet music at bit.ly/jl-sheet-music

Preview backing tracks at bit.ly/jl-backing-tracks

JOIN OUR COMMUNITY

to keep you growing as a flute player

Join a group of like-minded people who are passionately growing as flute players! Members of this Facebook group consists of only those who have worked with me 1:1, participated in a (virtual or live) workshop, worked with an online course or purchased sheet music or backing tracks.

Many of the members feel more comfortable in this smaller group to ask questions, posts videos of them playing and even finding an accountability partner so that you can tackle those obstacles in your flute journey!

facebook.com/groups/growingfluteplayer

AN EXPANDING LIBRARY

of videos for entertainment and education

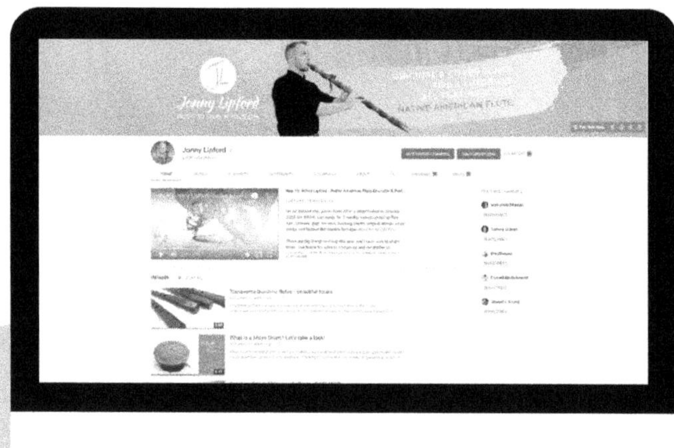

Immerse yourself in an ever-growing library of videos covering topics such as ***tips and tutorials, cover songs, original songs and flute reviews***. There are days of content here and I'm always adding more videos.

Grab your flute and tune in! While you're there, please consider subscribing!

SUBSCRIBE

www.ingramcontent.com/pod-product-compliance
Ingram Content Group UK Ltd.
Pitfield, Milton Keynes, MK11 3LW, UK
UKHW051134260726
13967UKWH00010B/3048